John F. Deane was born on Achill Island, Co Mayo, Ireland. He is the founder of Poetry Ireland, the National Poetry Society, and *The Poetry Ireland Review*. He is founder of the Dedalus Press, of which he was editor from 1985 until 2006. In 2006 he was visiting scholar in the Burns Library of Boston College, and in 2016 was Teilhard de Chardin Fellow in Christian Studies, Loyola University, Chicago and taught a course in poetry. In 2019 he was visiting poet in Notre Dame University, Indiana. His poems have been translated into many languages and in 2022 the Polish Publisher, Znak, published his *Selected Poems* in Polish translation. Deane is the recipient of many awards for his poetry, he is a member of Aosdána, the body established by the Arts Council to honour artists 'whose work has made an outstanding contribution to the arts in Ireland'. In 2007 he was made Chevalier en l'ordre des arts et des lettres by the French Government. The Cornish fine arts press, Guillemot, published a limited edition book, *Like the Dewfall*, in 2019, and in 2022 a further booklet, *Voix Celeste*, both with artwork by Tony Martin. In late 2022, Irish Pages Press published *Darkness Between Stars*, a selection of poems focusing on questions of faith and poetry by both John F. Deane and James Harpur, including an email dialogue on their individual writing processes. His latest collections from Carcanet are *Naming of the Bones* (2021) and *Selected and New Poems* (2023). In 2024, Guillemot Press published *The Red Gate* and, in 2025, Ura Forlag published a selection of poems translated into Norwegian by Jostein Sæbøe.

Also by John F. Deane from Carcanet

Toccata and Fugue (2000)
Manhandling the Deity (2003)
The Instruments of Art (2005)
A Little Book of Hours (2008)
Eye of the Hare (2011)
*Snow Falling on Chestnut Hill:
New and Selected Poems* (2012)
Semibreve (2015)
Dear Pilgrims (2018)
Naming of the Bones (2021)
Selected and New Poems (2023)

JONAH AND ME
JOHN F. DEANE

CARCANET POETRY

First published in Great Britain in 2025 by
Carcanet
Main Library, The University of Manchester
Oxford Road, Manchester, M13 9PP
www.carcanet.co.uk

ISBN 978 1 80017 524 2

Book design by Andrew Latimer, Carcanet
Typesetting by LiteBook Prepress Services
Cover Painting by John Behan, first published in *Achill, the Island*,
poems by John F. Deane, paintings by John Behan (Currach Press, 2018)
Printed in Great Britain by SRP Ltd, Exeter, Devon

MIX
Paper | Supporting
responsible forestry
FSC
www.fsc.org   FSC® C014540

The publisher acknowledges financial
assistance from Arts Council England.

Supported using public funding by
ARTS COUNCIL
ENGLAND

CONTENTS

CONSIDERING

EMERGENCE

TOWARDS VERSE

The valley lies still in the profound green
of late summer fullness. Scarcely a breath
on the air. Little expectancy. But the spirit
holds. There is much trouble in the world
but no diminution of hope, though the spring
acclamations of birdsong have been falling
silent. Quick mid-summer thunderstorms
have gone by. I have let the red gate swing
open to the demands of noon – in deep
shadows of the wood a smallest creature
stirs, hesitates; at the wood's edge, something
shifts amongst the grasses, falls still. Upstairs
the notebooks lie open, the laptop idles. I
pause a while, inhale, turn towards the house.

FOR WHOM THE BELL

AT SEA

Tonight I remembered – leaning lonesome
to the stove, with winds in the whining poplars

and rains splushing loud against the windows –
a summer day on Dooega beach, granny

in black, sitting, pensive, on a grey-dark rock
and watching as my favourite red ball

went bobboling away on the withdrawing tide –
her mind perhaps taken by a well-loved wayward son

lost to ships. There are, far out beyond the breakers,
the white-lightning scimitar dives of the gannets

down on their prey and, further out, the unheard
labouring of a small trawler; blue sky,

warm sand; long ago, too long for sorrow, so –
why this remembering now, why now?

NOTHING NEW

The winds come, knifing in over the árdán;
they shiver the whins, make me feel thin amidst them,
skinny, exposed, and cold;
'árdán', the book says: 'platform, hillock, mound'. A dog

barks, insistently, somewhere over the fields
and a donkey brays in the distance, a huge complaint;
camper-vans and caravans go by
and there, out beyond the village, the sea,

the abandoned pier and the crusty bones
of dried-out kelp. There is nothing new under the wind
here where bogland growth lies low,
hoarding its dark-blue bilberries, the lilac ling, the stonecrop

and though I am acquainted with these harsh winds, together
with the rains, the island's constancy and currency, now
I am shrivelling before them, stunted
like bush or tree, little shelter left. I shrug myself

deeper within my greatcoat, knowing old faith grows
to a knot of will and doubt, and I – old gentleman –
still schlep like a mountain goat that comes
clattering down, stone against stone and bone against bone.

PRESENCES

The beach at Keel curves away towards the cliffs
like a scythe; morning, I am scavenging

on the beach with the gulls, touch pebbles
and the broken shells of sea-lives. I choose

a rounded umber-coloured stone and marvel
at its guardianship of such millennia the mind

cannot assess. Yet we cherish memories of those
whom we have loved, strong essences the dead

bequeath to us. Nor do I stand alone, the mountains
rising behind me, the sea stretching to dim horizons.

THE MINAUN CLIFFS

That day the great
naves and archways of the Cathedral Rocks
collapsed into the sea;

ledge-nests of the razor-bill and guillemot
crumbled to dust; we had expected
eternity

from our cliffs and mountains but this was a death,
like so many other deaths and so unlike.
There were few

witnesses; a man and a woman, braving storm –
his lean-against-the-wind, her absolute clutch – declared
world's end. But world moves

in exquisite slow tempo, oceans gnaw
and the end is already there, hard packed,
in the beginning.

The hooded crows and the daws
held to their business, worrying
the blanched skulls of sheep; the couple –

his umbrella blown to a tanglement of spokes –
gathered stones to shape
love-initials across the grassy slope. And we

accepted, in our deepest bones, that this world
of rock and boulder
may be fragmented as easily

as bread that is broken.

FOR WHOM THE BELL

They were always a wonder to me – those
grown men in brown habits the shade
of algae, bladderwrack, sea dulse; white cinctures

like ropes holding them fast to the shore
against the draw of the winds and tides.
In the monastery, apart, they circled their Christ

who had circled them for years while the belfry
told the incarnation, warning of rocks and shoals.
But they were part of the stable shore. Like piers.

So, when the monastery died, the bell fell
silent; later, dropped through weakened timbers
and thudded onto earth where it stood,

in bronze solidity, a reproach. Beached. Now
the caws of crows still jangle in the trees. And the monks
have flown, a murmuration of angels, out to sea.

A HARVEST OF WHITE STONES

There was snowlight on the winter-hardened ground;

then, on a wind-shattered headland, I spoke your name –
Yeshua – you, water-walker;

I stood by the small humps of hungry grass,
one white stone for each lost child
and nobody on earth to know their names.

Across the harrowed ground of our many wars,
there will always be the planting of white crosses;

while I – by-the-wind-sailor John – am facing,
perhaps just a cry away, into my final birthing.

'To those who have come through,' the Spirit says,
'I will give a white stone, their name written secretly upon it'.

The centuries have grown virulent, and the soil weary.

I come to offer poems, petitionary, like prayers,
like small white stones
placed in rows on the winter-hardened ground.

THE BADLANDS

It was a door opening wide onto the world
from the confined systems of our concerns;

a place to dream, among soft, peaty acres,
easy to be secretive, as Nicodemus was,

slipping inside the house by night, seeking
understanding. To float on a world

brindled with heathers, water-lilies and the dream-coat
damselflies with their stained-glass blue twig-bodies;

to find oneself stilled within the great consciousness,
hushing a while the bleatings of the heart,

life radiant but disturbing, like the mind of Hopkins
in his days in Dublin. Human history here

is the dusk-light dawn-light miasma
of passing ghosts, where roots of the old forests

re-emerge from their deaths like mystic caravels,
with the dream of erecting a bothy out of scraws

and whin-sticks, of listening to the whispered music
of the winds, and of being one with the shriven earth.

COVERT

Rain falls, the big book says, on the unjust
and the just. Under a full moon the back yard
is a grainy, black-and-white old movie, fox
drifting from bin to compost heap, scraggling

a bone, chewing on rice-glumps, or licking
a plastic wrapper clean. Vixen has nowhere
to lay her head; I hear her, before dawn, return
from scavenging, scratch at her briar-bed;

under rainfall, sounds like hush-hush barking,
vixen-heart in its sorrowing. The fine red-gold
fur of fox is raw with mange. Once he let those
moon-eyes focus on me a moment, with disdain,

eyes all-emptiness, all-seeing. Mortal, like us all,
grace-filled, earth-weighted, greedy for being.

FRANCISCAN MONASTERY, ACHILL ISLAND

If, child, you arrive at dawn, at the monastery door
with the rooks raucous through the sycamores –
if you are unaware (as you *are* unaware)
of the turns and riddles of the roads ahead of you –
if you try to shuffle off the sleep, and keep
shrugging yourself deeper into the warmth of your coat –
you will slip into a hush and wholesomeness
before the lights about the altar and the brown-clad
bowed and cowled figures of the monks
wrapped in the aura of prayerfulness, and there
– in the soft centre of your being – the Saint himself
will glide into your consciousness and take possession,
so that later, when the roads have straitened and the years
raddled you, you will have thrown in your lot
with the itinerant Christ, seeking the fiery and fresh-cool
love the crucified demands, and with the *trovatore* who,
in summary foolishness, cumbered himself with Jesus,
bodily, in the flesh, and sang off-key and heartfully
of the holiness of all creation, of rook and sycamore,
of monk and schoolboy, till you too would be knight,
jongleur and chorister in the service of the Christ – so
be watchful for the skylarks, for peace upon the world,
searching for ways to help repair God's tumbledown house,
and then, when you come back, at noon, you will find
peace, and silence, ocean distantly breathing, breezes
sighing absence so you find yourself whelmed to know
how you too have loved this earth, that now you may turn
to find the cemetery, with its small, arrayed coterie
of saints, where the plaque says *Welcome Sister Death*, you

part of it all, how people everywhere have been quickening beautiful as light while radiance comes to you still from star and planet, and the bracing sky is brightening, so you cannot say they failed, for here the precise need ended, as Jesus, awkwardly taken from the cross, was not a failure; and at last you arrive on the verge of prayer, aware how the compassionate love of our God is extravagant, transcending all belief.

OF HUMAN FLESH

A sequence, in several
voices, for Holy Week

The Rushy Field (Wednesday)

Time, again, to confess, but this time, not
lusts of the flesh nor pride of life, but to cherishing
the embodied: like those dawdling dandelions
along the roadside and their glowing in hazy sunshine,
or how the old man stands, compassionate
in the rushy field, lights a fag, and coughs,

and gobs, and how the ewes are gathering to him
like schoolchildren, as he turns towards the gate,
muttering each individual name, and they follow,

trustful, towards the truck. If you crouch down here
close to the ground, where ewes and lambs have been
separated, you may see the delicate scarlet flowers
of the pimpernel, and high on the enclosure wall,
thriving on the dustiest pinch of dust, the littlest
bride-white blossoms of the chickweed.

A Sea of Troubles: The Nun's Story
My shepherd is the Lord.

I grow impatient for an outcome –
thou wouldst not think how ill's all here –
no matter; days we ingest half-truths

when I distrust both word and gesture,
when even the holiest cloistered sister
appears to hesitate against the altar. Prayer
wanes, now and in Ireland, and the house
is withering around me – though once I dreamed
of a fine, exemplary death. Today I refused

the Hours and stayed outside, past matins,
past lauds and prime, chanting snatches
of old airs to thrush and buttercup

in sunlit torpor, 'til cries of the noonday
schoolgirls roused me. Mine a petulant
betrayal, hinting – they said – dementia.

Sins of the Fathers: The Nun's Story (Thursday)

They taught me guilt, Adamchild, inheriting.

I stuttered to the age of reason, dropped to my knees in big-
box-dimness, whispering *Father, for I have sinned*: child-eva-
sions, truancies, small filches.

Today in the common-room, the TV showed a child of
Yemen, not yet three, so much of suffering he has no lungs
to scream, the doctors cannot find a vein in that needle-thin
body.

I wept for him, of human flesh, who is all of the children,
face pressed to the hard earth of Gethsemane;

perhaps we, I pray, who have pleaded for him in his agony,
are the angel who came to comfort him, leaving the merest
brush of a kiss across his sweat-soaked brow.

Nazareth House: the Upper Room

Missionaries, long retired, they were in the day-room;
sunshine lay amongst them, like grandmother's old cat;

someone had gathered bluebells and late narcissi
and stood them in a glass bowl by the microphone;

apostles, sluggish with walkers or seated stiffly
in straight-backed chairs or wheelchairs; Sister

handed out a clutch of the old songs and they sang,
patched and trembly voices weakly willing: *Memories*

are made of this, Lily of the Lamplight, The parting glass.
And one, dribbling a little, head drooped over a soiled

bib, who had been tall amongst them, giving everything
of himself, was whispering to the air, soft spittle-words.

This patient, attendant mass of men, with their charts
of pains and their exotic ailments, have no quarrels

with their lives. The day-room, sacred space, mead-hall,
these old men, shrunken and wearied through, these

chosen ones, are made whole, the way the heritage
crimson rose unfolds in Christ across cosmic mystery.

Night into Morning: The Nun's Story

Night lengthens out across Great Silence;
I do not sleep;
my quiet Lord demands immensities; I read
from *Revelations*, John, the dream with the heavenly city

showing crystal clear;
there is comfort in the words, the vision,
angels at the great gates, guarding.
I watch the moon as it labours across the night,

and know the determined growth of the earth
as my body is diminishing.
I will slide close to the point of utter loneliness,
that emptiness, the Beloved unresponding.

I, too, have grovelled, pleading; in these cloisters
once crowded with the presence of the absolute Creator,
the Christ at night; now not a board creaks,
original faith diminishing.

The Evangelist, John (Friday)

Golgotha: earth's loneliest outcrop, crag of violence.
I see, under the yew trees, where the sequestered sisters
– long gone to their bridegroom Christ – lie still,

bluebell, celandine and saxifrage are flourishing again;
I, John, hold to man's son, cruelly assaulted,
who is undergoing still the worst humanity can inflict.

I, John – though it was two thousand years ago, and I –
stones for bones – remember as if it was yesterday:
forenoon of extreme suffering, starting early,

the mockery, the spitting, the slapping.
In the barracks yard, grit coarsening the ground,
they flayed him, a day sun-washed, patched and pitted;

basins sluiced the blood down into the gutters.
He, of human flesh like all of us, was pitiful,
you could see spine and ribs, and he fell, in torment,

sustained only by the ferocity of his love.
Nearby, bazaars were raucous with their bargaining,
stalls laden with scents and shadows,

ordinary wine, breads on offer in the booths.
I was there. I watched him. He cried out, and died.
Here was standstill, source and seed, centred on the wood.

Stillest point of space and time, a mouth
of utterance, a profound pool of Being. Yet
no word of reproof was uttered from the cross.

Attente de Dieu: The Nun's Story (Saturday)

Slow day. Slow afternoon, long drag
into dusk; fasting and inadequate prayers
have dried up all my bones; from the window
I look down on small allotments, labours of the poor,
neat ridges humped, like grave-mounds.

In our nuns' garden everything is still;
the dead, always close to me, crowd out
my dreams, and nightmares. I fret
under the long waiting.
Slow day. Slow evening. I watch,

in the quiet chapel, the candles, one by one,
gutter and go out. The slaughtered body,
in flight on the stylized cross, will not lift
the spirit out of the valley of dry bones.
Last light filters slowly

through the maryblue high window;
I am in darkness utterly, heavy
with niggardly efforts to love. Long night,
and slow. And shall I turn, like the Magdalene,
startled into certainties, into love unstinted?

The Afterlife: The Nun's Story

This morning they found me, virgin
from the Song of Songs, would-be bride
of a doubtful Hamlet, out in the dawn-light
in my convent night-gown. I crouched close
to the spring earth outside the walls
where the great wheels of articulated trucks
ravage the roadside verge. I found the delicate
blossoms of the primrose and I am one with them,
and one with the constellations in their turning
far above. Perhaps I suffered an excess of mind,
being desolate now, here in this once populated
city. Body's seeds are of human flesh; soul,
that soars over the stones of this world, is
of God. I am consoled by the beauty
of the ditch orchid, hurt by loss of the skylark,
defeat of the yellowhammer and the corncrake;
I groan at the world's betrayal of the children.
The good sisters came and picked me off the ground,
tut-tutting, but I know something necessary
is set to happen, something beyond the beyondness
of belief. Amen, amen! Father, into your hands.

The Lamb (Sunday)

April is the disentangling month; an old man,
standing in a rushy field, pointed out our way,

between motorway and high-speed railway-line
a few rough acres of neglected ground; we walked,

the sun being risen, among earth-mounds
and straggling furze, stones and leaning alders;

beneath us the long-ago buried Vikings
who sailed upriver and left their bones. We crossed

under the motorway, in the stench of sheep-shit
and bat-droppings, and came out among stalks

of withered thistles, outcrops, merds; easy here,
where sheep scurry away, to know vexation of spirit

in a country left to wrack. One ewe had straggled
away from the flock, heaving, her wool snagged;

she lay, eyes huge, and panting; when we looked again
there, as if suddenly, was the lamb, wet with new

being, staggering and nuzzling, stick-legs
all-bendable, wool dyed with birthing. World moves

in starts and fits, with its greenfinches, its daffodils,
with darksome swirls in the river-water. But all here fits

together, oxbow and pillow-stone, holon and fractal,
stunning, admonishing, this morphogenic field.

CONSIDERING

HOUSE OF CARDS

The dead are gathering again round the parlour table;
they have shaken the snow from their great-coats,

scraped off the boot-clay and settled down to a night
of poker: chemist and parish priest, doctor

and country nurse, with father and mother
hosting. The child on the staircase, listening,

hears – and oh! so many years ago – the laughter,
the clinking of coins on the table, the chink

of cut glass. Behind that door there will be
smoke from cigarette and pipe, a gold-white

and warm-bronze glow from the firelight
on whiskey, brandy, and sherry-glass. At times

the boy will hear the shuffle-fall of the turf
and what the music of that night will have told:

of the not-now, the yet-to-come wonderful;
but for now, only a pencil-thin line of light

under the parlour door, and what the child won't know
– not yet – of the pendulum insistence on ash

and boot-clay, of the joys and sorrows of the house
of cards, of the young boy's eyes slushed with sleep.

TRUSTING IN WONDERS

To step out from the gunwale onto water, that
is unreasonable or, like the apostle – who had been
sitting lost in thought under a fig-tree – to leap

suddenly out of one's comfort and follow a stranger
down a rutted, trouble-fretted path: that, too,
is unreasonable. But we must live in trust, day

upon day, and so – set down the baby's name
on fine parchment: boy-child, Nathaniel John;
bless the ears with fragrant oils, the breast,

the forehead; enrol him in the precious company
of the blessed and loving, the cared-for and
the caring. Cosmos, we know, is a forest of hazels,

each hazelnut a universe; so if, in the morning,
the wind comes whistling its chaos-songs
in under the door, trust to the day's lightening,

honour an unfussed belief in the best the human
heart can aspire to; the waters will bear him up, winds
will ease, kind hands will reach for him should he fall.

for Nathaniel Leonard

AS ONE

We are carrying our death about with us –
deep in the oesophagus, perhaps, attendant,
or in the folds and furrows of the brain. And though
conscious of God's unseasonable demands
we admit to our unreasonable responses.
                                    Today
insistent mists are holding the countryside enthralled,
while tulips, in sundry vivid colours, bow low
in fragile reverence; and I think: sometimes God
holds us tenderly on her upturned palms.
                              Perhaps
mine may be a sea-death or, more likely, a road,
when God will lay her iron-solid world-weight down
on the tenders of my days. But knowing there are wars
and time-worked earth-disasters, still I watch – trusting
to the drive of compelling cosmic forces – the orchid,
the upward-uncoiling fern,
                        while I remember the three
Palestinian children – who had been playing ball
by the sea-shore – blown into shreds and bone-bits
by the state-of-the-world Israeli fighter jet: they
had carried their death about with them for too short
a time and – though we know that barbarism
divides us, soul from soul – we, hurting, cry out
as one, in the woodshed, the cow-byre, in the high
-rise offices of the city: have you abandoned us!

THE INNER ROOM

Deep in the inner room I have been for years
stravaging, leaving it mightily cluttered; millennia,
hidden in non-being, I have slept, and will be
dropped again, into the mess. But – for now and here –

I walk a long and twisting lane, enjoying
golden leaves, fingerbone twigs, ultimate reality
always at unbridgeable distances. Sometimes
I have found myself elated, watching the friskiness

of a perfectly formed black lamb just fallen
from its mother, flinging itself about as if it owned
the whole rush-laden field it was born to, so now,

delighting in the irreversible force that drives
the seasons, I do not regret the spirit's edginess
in the clutter-room, distracted from the everlasting.

PROPITIOUS PLACES

Look! – in the wild garden – what a fellowship
of startling orchids; and there –

by the neglected footpath, see!
a gallery of high and silken grassheads, whisperish;

and this, too:

in loveliness, over by the graveyard wall,
lupin is choiring, silently, upwards.

These days the spirit
wanders, ghostly, bewildering always – halts

by the sacred places, thin-partitioned,
earth brushing the heavens, the netherworld gate –

while we –

we take ourselves in hand, watchful,
going round and round them, listening.

LATE LULLABY

I had drawn you to the scents of our beloved earth,
buddleia, sweet pea, the briar rose… Then, this first
morning, I watched you walk, half-run, towards

big school, bearing your new bag of many colours,
pristine books, pencils and parer, a bright lunch-box…
You passed the early autumn blackthorn, its bitter

glossing sloes, and the hawthorn, its hawberry fruits,
while, from the front gardens, sun-gold rudbeckia
and high-flamingo cosmos were waving gently

in the breeze: and I remembered sitting by your cot,
not long since, singing softly, over and over, Brahm's
Wiegenlied: *Lay thee down now and rest, Lullaby*

and God bless, praying you ever guarded by the angels;
you drifted, like a star, slowly into dreams
while on the city's back-yard corrugated shed-roofs

cats prowled and hunted, yowling – so now I wish you
light, confidence in the sustaining presence of love,
to know your name written green on our illimitable earth.

for Thomas Leonard

A CHILD'S BUSINESS

The sea was wild about the skerries, the breakers
pounded against the harbour walls; baby
not yet in position, unwilling to venture
into our world – Russian forces massed on borders

with Ukraine. At my feet one perfect yellow crocus
stood in stiff grass while a bumble-bee, too early,
probed the unyielding carpel. I remembered
the wildering violence of the Atlantic, how the ocean

flings itself against cathedral rocks, that point
where eternity and time struggle in entanglement;
white foam shivering on the gothic arches, sea-birds
chorusing in the side aisles. Perhaps you could glimpse,

if your eye shone clear, beyond the rock-fall, and
for just a moment, the creating forces of original God.

When baby grew to six months old, I lifted him,
grandchild, Edward, delighting to swing him high,
and he held me suddenly with his enchanting eyes,
knowing me as I am known; I was stunned to see

into the Everything he has come from, those inflexible,
long reaches of time, galaxies in the fiery embrace
of their birthing, and their annihilations. I have learned,
in my turns and returns, that my God is nothing,

that Edward and I are less, and I know, too, that we
are everything, shear-water and altar stone, rose,
greenfly and lady-bird, we are star-matter, light,
lichen of dark forests, cry of dinosaur and tread

of black-boot soldiers, lilies of the field and the free
enchanting song-birds of the woods and hedgerows.

for Edward Leonard

CALVIN

The earth goes rolling slowly towards her rest,
one monumental wave out of the cosmic sea
bearing on its back the glory of its flotsam,
welcoming in its depths the wrecks, the jetsam;
it bears the small things, too, the Himalayas and the fjords,
detritus of back gardens and high-rise offices;

and cats, of course,
the Persian, the Manx, the Munchkin;
wicked cats too, the meanest, mangiest cat anchorites.

Brother loved a cat,
one spiteful, big, self-ostracising cat,
brother adopted him, and he adopted brother.
Cat would hiss and spit against the world, with a
screechy sideways hop, his shabby coat
standing erect on his off-black high-arching back,
should you presume –

while brother struggled years with his own demons, grew skilled
in subterfuge but fought against himself and won.

The cat (whom he named Calvin)
snuggled in to him and he hugged the cat
close to his heart.

Calvin, he said, reminded him
of life's bazaars, of spitfires, pantries, crab-apples, wasps.

When they laid my brother in his wooden box,
dressed in his pearl-pure chasuble and stole,
they placed a silver-fine small crucifix close to his heart,
and at his side, in a Nordic urn, they left the ashes
of his cat Calvin.

In the cemetery in Pleasant Hill
we heard a purring sound as the casket-lowering device
laid them gently down together into eternity.

i.m. Declan Deane

ON THE MOUNTAIN HIGH

In the beginning was nothing, nothing orthodox, nothing
unorthodox. Only the pure point of utterness
out of which are all things disposed. Still – from the mountain-top

you could see the Everything: south,
the island villages, the fields and wildscapes, teeming life;
east: the mainland, its confusing folds and fallows,

its humped horizons. To the west: the Ocean,
stunning in its wilderness and bounty, the ruck of islands vanishing
in haze; and north: Atlantic boundlessness, beyond and beyond,

the mesmerizing dance of distances and the harmony
of things that are not.
If you stood, carefully, holding your balance and looking up,

you could see the clouds, the heavens and cosmos, possibility
of worlds past worlds, beyond thinking. We,
brothers and young, conquerors already, were relishing

breezes about our ears and the high whistle of a kestrel
in blues that were shading towards silver. We stretched our arms wide
encompassing the island, our care and holding,

and then set off, down and down, air-inebriated,
the leaps, the falls, the laughter;
he and I, fresh-water and blood-grouped, never to be separated, we

immortals, and how wonderful it would be,
to soar out, sustained on the broad arms of utterness,
together, over the waves, to be filled full, to be made whole.

MIDWINTER

I have this news for you: we have come back,
under the fug of a pandemic, to a heartiness
of fields and hedgerows, to our shabby-genteel
slow-stepping pheasant, and our fine-tuned

red squirrels ousting finches from the feeders;
we have come back to sacred space, to January airs
and embracing silence. On the low hills, under
a chilling fog, there are brittle nests of snow,

appearing overnight like unspeaking, seasonal
migrants, hidden amongst dead ferns, scrawny
grasses side of the road, melt-water guttering. So,

after the many sorrows, we hold this world still
to our hearts. But your loss has left me hanging,
like water-pearls on the bars of the red gate.

BETWEEN WORLDS

We had stories still to tell, stories now that can have
      no ending, like our gleeful jumping into puddles

as we, free as eagles, relished the splish-splosh dance
      of the senses, the two of us together

bound to the earth in peacock-coloured squeaking
      wellingtons, innocent yet of the need for bridges

or the suggestions of fingerboards, we, children, flowing
      as water flows, two hand-holding ego-hoops of joy,

long before the alcohol and the addiction, long before
      the scorpions had nested in your throat, we

once-upon-a-time word-tasters, truths to be sourced
      and sounded, to be blooded forever between us.

And then, in our sleaky, homemade boat, out
on the lake, we both fell silent, the oars, lifted

and dripping water on the surface, soft, softly,
something incomprehensible holding us, fragrance

breathing from the heathers, the low hills embracing,
and lake-water tapping gently against the timber bones

of the craft: we drifted, a long sustaining moment
in unannounced communion, as childhood drew

nearer to the rough-rock shores and our leaning bodies
grew firmer towards the tasks ahead; until

we rowed again, oars raking against the rowlocks, silence
persisting deep within us, swelling to a form of prayer.

THE ROUGH-ROCK SHORE

The Clare Island light has gone out;
on the darkest night it swept slowly round the bay
with insistent reassurance;

I am standing now
where all that I can see is a white lace hem
on the black waves, and knowing that

out there, across the oceans,
there are rubber dinghies of refugees
stalked by the sharks of empire. Tonight,

a murmuring encouragement
sounds in the regular irregular shushing of surf
while the foreshore offers disharmonies

in the shifting of stones across the undertow.
The lone contralto call of a sea-bird
somewhere out in darkness, is all of life I know

at this moment, in this place. Do you remember,
brother, how we stood sad together
where the Killeen holds in its dark and sandy soil

the misprized children, those exiled generations
for whom we still mourn,
we who have lived long, and in the light?

In the high branches of the eucalyptus, a blackbird
watches, waiting; I, too, hold still by the window,
lingering. The lupins, that stood high in pride,
are wilted now, assuming the sadder aspects of age;
all of us, waiting, in silence. Yet within me

there is agitation, lest I miss the words I hope for,
your words of clarity and definition, as your death
resolved a reticence that had lain between us. Now
shadows drift, hugely, towards me; world turns
on the smallest of pinions, soundless. So, call to me,

brother, from within the light that flickers
somewhere near the heart: but not as a dream flickers,
goes out and is forgotten – call to me in a silence
so intense it burns, leaving a certainty that will transmute,
over the remaining years, into the end of longing.

Everything holds neat in the meadows of Elysium, light
spreading radiance like a presence, with a glad-sad ruc-
tion of bright grave-flowers, bronze pots and gaudy rain-
bow-painted windmills, while extensive peace dreams
down from the low mountains, shaded sunset rose. Those
of us who have lived with demons stalking us close as
consciousness, who have fought them hopelessly, need
companion ghosts: like those that spirited our badlands
beneath Slievemore, back on the island, those sun-kissed
cuttings, where no bell rings and skylarks soar, where we
startled a flock of peewits that burst into the air and a
sparrow-hawk, like a flash of fire, slewed away with a sharp
disappointed cry. That was an unruly world but it was ours
and beautiful, where we leapt from tump to hummock and
never dreamed diminishment, its wash, its purifying pow-
er. Whisper to me now, as the delicate flowers of bog-as-
phodel are hushed under the breeze, breathe to me as the
wind that eases down from the slopes of Mount Diablo, as
it stirs here, across your resting-place.

GO, SAID THE BIRD

I was standing, still, just inside the gate, testing
the echo of some yelp or yawp I could not identify,
somewhere from the larches and clustering pines,
a call that drifted on the air, like a messenger's
whose speech was slurred and incomprehensible;
I was seeking, as always, some form of sanctuary
for the dithering fancies of the mind. Now I was
startled by a croak low-pitched and ragged, and saw
the bird, wide-winged, lethargic, its irritating caw
commonplace and dreary as it flopped, gawkily, down
onto the parapet, closed its wings and posed: parsonly –
heron. The water that came flowing down the culvert
was shallow, sluggish and the high brick wall
of the reservoir was marbled a slimy green; I sensed
the baleful cobra-eye of the charcoal-dark preacher
fixed on me, alien to his territory; till he flapped
up, with an impatient squawk, and dropped, more
cautiously, to the edge of water, then stabbed down
into the wet. A breeze came, teasing from the pine-trees,
I shivered a moment till that arcane dread of portents
eased from me. Suddenly a deer, small and fleeing,
leapt from the trees and I knew from the yapping
of a foppish, hearth-trained lapdog, a human presence
was somewhere by. I sighed, irritated with myself –
I have learned that the dead will not speak to the living,
between us a gulf, dark, uncharted, is death to cross.
I closed the gate and started up the rough-stone track.

THE CORNICHE CARRIAGE CLOCK

A sequence: for Cyril
O'Regan

Marriage of Jeremiah Deane and May Brosnan, 8 May 1897,
Listowel, Co Kerry
Marriage of John Connors and Nora O'Malley, 16 February
1906, Westport, Co. Mayo
Marriage of Mary Connors and Donal Deane, 1 June 1940,
Westport, Co Mayo

A French Corniche Carriage Clock with an 8-day Timepiece
A little reminder of happy and instructive hours spent with
C.S.M.I. Connors
from No.3 Squad. 24th Rifle Class, S. of M.
Dollymount 1916

The grove has been long lost, though extant in memory —
prime, majestic

               breathfilled in breeze and storm
                    flushed in off the Atlantic

I have climbed back up the knobbled bark and branches
to sit high and solitary

               content, watchful

like a sated harrier, in a crotch of bark and bole
one with the time, and times, the root and canopy

one with the ragged mat of ochre-dull pine-needles
and the soft moistening of persistent rains

where I am isolate, companion to the winds
hidden under the everyday, a barren air-scape

               sky-wide

in the delighting scent and stickiness
of dark-gold resin on the hands
                    animal, mineral

*

The Scots Pine Grove

Time past, passed in the Scots Pine grove,
was a listening, child-heart, to the trees, their soft-sift
mysterious whispering

                         with the snow falling
and thickening the air, till you could imagine a measured
hosting of phantoms through the murk, the layers

                   of pine-needles on the earth
stiffening in the chill.

                   Where I sat, nested high
and sheltered among the branches, I knew a muddled
melancholy and delight, sensing something of the loneliness

of the soul:
              being already that old man who would be
              holding memory of the child I was,

                   time a mere deception –

as the soft hooting of the owl that will shade the killing
of a lightsome creature, vole or shrew or fieldmouse,

foraging among the ravellings below.

             *

In Retrospect

The way round the field of wonder was to creep-crawl
on your knees, splendid in the rhododendron hedge,

through otherworlds of shadowy importance and satisfying
risks; to be amongst the secret creatures, the creepers,

the eye-bright, the burrowers; no mercy sought, you ventured
bravely, everything against you, you – hero, and victor.

Pause:

and know the heart thumping, the attar of furze-petals opening,
the squeaky-clean hubbub of the world turning. For one discreet

animating hour, you were not who you had to be, there was only
faithfulness to the project, flesh pricked by thorns, your *geansaí*

an unravelling of threads. Now age has leached the animality
from the field but cleaves still to those days that hold a light

and chequered importance, the dreams that come ahead
of cares, and history from the brightly-coloured storybooks.

*

Turf

The bank we laboured on was deep, from heather-scraw
down to the blackest waters; it held the histories
of winds and rains, of bog-oak roots, and the slow, slow
passing of the centuries; in its original darkness the peat

guarded a hoard of knowledge, but we worked and pillaged,
moulding turves to warm for a while our western bones,
cherishing the flicker of flames that eased the evenings,
the murmurings of shifting sods and ash that told

of the falling away of time. We found no golden torcs
but have always valued the contorted forms of turf,
like stored memories, like dreams of Ireland. Dusk
we, restful around the hearth, counted our beads, rehearsed

the sacred mysteries, and the great wrongs done to us.

*

About Time

It's a question of time, the irritating ticking of the carriage
clock while you try to focus on 'I am'... Still, when you do

shimmy into God's presence, God shimmies into yours;

when you touch on quiet, your name written, you may hear
God's murmuring – although you have not yet quite learned

the language; when you watch a summer sunset turn from
rose to damson, you will know a pianissimo air is being played

on the strings of a cosmic violin, though your ears are not yet
quite attuned to it; you remember those who have flown over

into that music and have learned the Maestro's handling,
you sense their gossiping and gaiety, how they cavort around

you, your heart ringing. For you it's a question of time, the was
of being, the now of presence, the coming-to-be of absence.

*

Ah, Bright Wings

Today the sky
            turned a sea-glass green, the sea
was the thrush-egg blue of the sky;

nearby the mountain river played
            a boulder music over the steepest falls;

in a stiff wind
            the bog-brown water in the lake
flung high small storms of butterfly-white froth;

I was wondering if the eels –
        the way pennants flutter in a breeze –
were wiggling their stringy clean-gold bodies

to hold their place in the disturbed disturbing
waters, when an insect, size of a full stop

landed on my page, paused, touched on the word
        'intent', then
(mind of its own, bones, heart, lungs) lifted away

into the air: pilgrim, too, Odysseus
over this bewildering and phenomenal creation.

                            *

Of Light and Darkness

I hear now, through the window, the breaking waves
of a high tide; the moon drops a long
shivering track across the sea and all of the bay
lies calm and peaceful;
                            I cannot sleep, I am gripped
by a time long past, of darkness and light, world,
closed and static, faithful, and *doloroso*;

beyond the city's lights, the spaciousness of cosmos,
beyond and beyond, unfathomable;

there is a gloom encompasses me, root and stalk,
a fear the Christ might well

       not be so, not at the core
of this awful process, and that, our fire out,
we will melt like sods of ash back into earth.

They were frightening, the sean-bheans, ancient
as Slieve More, and as hacked,
with words of affection only for the animals
as the buckets clattered; once

       they gathered in the front room,
grandfather coffined down in the cold parlour;
the sean-fhears too, stubbled dark and watchful,

chewing on the stems of white-clay pipes, swallowing
porter from the bottle and gulping down fists
of whiskey; men on one side, women
on the other, and I, scarce ten years old

       tending them. *Lacrimosa,*
the infolded room, bleak light from
high candles and smoky, faltering oil-lamps.

Those days the women's calls were cries of the hooded crow
from the high reaches; twig-fashioned broom
to sweep boy and goose out of the hen-shitted yard;
and one road-wanderer

       hoisted her fardel of skirts
and let her Shannon flow freely on the cart road;
those days the men, with talk of weathers and stiffening

bones, with odour of shed and stable, grey stains
on the Sunday suit, were deft with the old brown

kitchen knife to cleave the head
off a cocky hen;
                              old men, old women,
in laceless black boots and grey woollen stockings,
faithful to the Mother of a recalcitrant son Jesus.

I cannot sleep; I am penned in; there is darkness
even where there is light; I fear unfaith, its
stone certainties. Time hurries on; it harries us.
There is a cruise-ship, a city en fête,
                              easing itself smoothly out
on the Irish Sea; we have come far, but a life
strains towards light and spaciousness, rest for the soul.

                              *

The Entangled Bank

It soothes me, the high, uneven stone ditch,
greened over with lichens and moss, where a concrete

pillar holds the hinges of the garden gate: beyond –
the garden, potatoes in regimented drills, offering

their wistful blooms. He gathers stones, almost
boulders, and in gaps and cavities, the soil

accumulates dead leaves and seeds until the wall
is a wildflower wonderment, vetch and bindweed,

shy violet, pimpernel, with curious robins singing
in the trees, vole and fieldmouse secretive in the cracks.

I see myself clambering over, relishing this
Darwin's delighting entangled bank and, within me,

sense of the mystery, its everyday miracle and hallows.
I see him, in soiled vest, braces stretched over muscle

and back, stoop, lift, placing the heavy stones, one by one,
and building. Grandmother calls, they are lovers, the century

turning; it is spring forever, the golden hyacinth is blooming
on the compost heap. The ditch is flawed, letting energy flow,

letting wildness find its lovely way through. Grandfather sees
that it is good. It will do, he says, and I smile, knowing.

*

The Carriage Clock

Tread softly here; he lies ill; ill-tempered, too;
pray for him, urgently, soft-whispering.
Saturdays, 8 o'clock, the old man lifted the carriage clock
from its place of honour, mantelpiece, centre,

opened the glass door at the back, fitted the brass key,
wound, anti-clockwise, counting aloud,

nine turns; hung the key back, replaced the clock:
all regular, slow march, about turn, stand at ease. That

was long ago; time is unforgiving, the mighty fortresses
come tumbling down. Tiny dewdrops
on his yellowing moustache, he lived a little apart, old-style,
Constabulary. Royalist, out of favour. We are not lost,

she will say, the old woman who took her loneliness
to heart; we, she will say, are small people, ordinary
with our small fields and hedgerows, our lives
hidden with Christ in God. And yes, I loved him,

she will say, with his brass buttons, his bicycle clips,
his gruff tenderness. We are forgiven, and we
forgive. At times, she will say, out of her grief,
even Father, Son and Holy Ghost may ask forgiveness.

*

The Barracks

The village, a scatter of poorer houses. 'Tóin
an tSean-Bhaile', back-side of the old home-place;

                        the R.I.C., "royal" though no
king or queen, prince or princess had ever hiked this way;

it was files, blue ink out of an ink-pot, blots on the page;
nothing shattering: cattle loose, lamps on bicycles –

the ocean surf hummed a soothing song on the rare
sunshine days,

               but there was the sweat of damp
on the dark-green walls, turf half-smoking in the grate.

The lighthouse across the bay was comfort in the long
lonesome evenings; stars were whelming in their abundance

and the terrible longevity at their core;
                    to be part of this

however minuscule, was, in itself, magnificence;
to love, be loved, he knew, is worth beyond all, but he

did not have the words, the telling gestures. Irishman –
resented and resenting, he went into exile:

                  London, Birmingham,

came home when the noise died down. History, we know,
corrodes, the way the ocean gnaws at the roots of rock.

               *

Grandmother

There is a time for war, the Book says and she
was intimate with war, each with its seasons
serving the interests of the small, whimpering gods;

intimate, too, with death, her missal swollen
with cards: sons, daughter, husband, the dead with their
smiling faces, with their dispatches from beyond

where love and violets thrive. When grandfather died
she let the carriage-clock, with her expectations, wind
down, and stop. This, too, is love; oh sleeping Lord,

do you not see, hear, how we hurt? Now, where I write
a winter storm is complaining in the chimney;
I have been gifted the corniche carriage clock, have

wound it up again, inheriting its ticking, its ritual
remembering, the sorrow, the righteousness, the love.

*

I sit at peace, near the irregular
breathe-in breathe-out of the Irish Sea,
focusing on the difficult task
                    of prayer;

decades back, I came climbing down
from my green nesting high in the pines,
child-heart unknowing that I was present
                    with grandfather God

and that the Christ-child had been seated by me.
In these my earthbound years I hurt
for the cut daffodils that open their hearts
                    in a glass jar

on the pantry shelf; hurt for the lambs,
spring in their steps, purified
for the Easter seasoning; world, tree
                    and carriage clock,

all of this, the full heart hopes, is Eucharist;
with all of time and memory,
flesh-bread and blood-wine, matter –
                    dusk filling

the felled pines, the lingering scent of resin and decay,
animal, mineral, convergent pattern
and impetus of this sanctuary cosmos.

JONAH AND ME

WHITETHORN

Could be it never had beginning,
lone bush, may bush, hawthorn;
woods and forests round have disappeared,

it is Sphynx, still haughty, still abrupt;

now it broods on ancient secrecies
under the curious watch of the moon
and the drifting slowly over

of the wistful stars. Like old Ireland
with its hearths, its haws and its slow
processional white returns of the May,

its spirits have gone to ground

along with penances of the Skellig monks;
it looms, thorny intertwining limbs
shielding the wren; rears up big as a hayrick,

cocky as a temple dome – self-righteous.

Could be that now in this cyborg age
the little people, affrighted, have ceased
their unholy jigs and reels around it. So

I cannot cut it down; it will stand,
with its deities, its Ferguson, its Yeats,
font of faithfulness, portal to wonder.

THE HIGH POPLARS

These February days the poplars are making
their soft gossiping sounds; they rise, three together,
steeple-tall, a scraggy trinity, standing side by side
and swaying in the winds as one; their roots

will link them close to kith and kin across the fields,
entangle in a system like the Roman catacombs,
radicles to sustain each other while their lowest branches
mesh as if they clutched at one another, for sustenance.

I stand, congregation of one, to honour the trees'

serenity, their grasp of the ultimate realities
that never leave them in perplexity. I would share
their wisdom, their labouring, haughty and raw
against coming storms, but they – when spring

shivers the earth again – will gather to themselves
fresh and fulsome dresses towards the weatherfull
gladnesses of summer. Mine is to murmur the old
gnarled prayers, my limbs stiffening like twigs.

WAKENING

He found the body gross, like mutton-fat,
the mind sour, as buttermilk, as crud.
Now he wakes with dawn, still in darkness,

grown old, bones creaking like a grating door.
Sometimes he feels like the farmyard mutt
useless on three legs, all straggling hairs;

what wisdom he bears is useless as a shadow,
eyes lifeless as pond-water. But he has settled
to a comforting placidity. Prayer is silence,

spirit-bones and soul-blood fluctuant as breath.
He moves towards the judgment-door, and –
though humankind has mapped the galaxies,

filled grains of sand into a glass and called it
time – he knows the young man Lazarus fell asleep
and Jesus, weeping, slowly moved to waken him.

JONAH AND ME

I was reading in the Big Book: Baalam's donkey,
Elisha and Naaman, the leper cured, and gratitude –
I thought of Jonah, my Bunnacurry mule, big and raw,
stubborn in hardship and unwilling, insistent

in calling out from his knowledge of the world, wise
in his own way, as Solomon. We stood together,
wearied, out on the wide spaces of the bogland,
honey-scent of heather on the breeze, in a quietude

that could be prayer. The high dome of the sky
was a mystic blue, and somewhere in the low growth
of rush and scraw, a pipit sang; beyond the ridge
of the low hills, the Atlantic Ocean sounded, its soft

regular shushing of the breakers like a breathful
hymn of praise. It was as if we were standing, lone,
in the first church, we – the first worshippers, awed
and wordless. I had filled the salley creels on either

side of Jonah, from the footings dried in the sun
where the peat-thickened water wallowed dark
from the deep veins of earth, and we started back,
Jonah and me, good companions. The bog road

was rough with stone and sorrow, and we, Jonah
and me, moved in a slow, uncomely cosmic dance
of bemused fellowship. We stopped: I took two sods
from either creel and carried them, to ease his load,

thanking him and flinging away my stick; kindly
I laid my hand on the unshaven and twitching rump
and sensed the stone-like bones of his spine, then
we carried on, Jonah and me, towards our Nineveh.

THE HARMONIES

Amos said that when God calls
a prophet has no choice but to answer, to tell how the nations
must hold this perishable earth, passionately,
within their hearts;

alone on the sloblands I heard the curlews
call in meshed cacophony and the lapwing chant their startling
pee-wit hymn, all part of the regular irregular
harmonies of the Atlantic,

and because I know how we will be old
but for a time, I pray that the poems singing themselves
out of the soul's sanctum, may offer a dulcet, difficult music,
perhaps relevant, like prophesy.

THE LIVING CREATURES

And if that motorbike, veering and swerving, should have
crash-ploughed into me – bodysoft and bone-frail – as I leapt to

avoid it, and if bike and rider and I
should have been smashed and slithered along

for yards and for yards across the road and flung
to a shuddering mess-up of glass and shards, of oil, limbs

and loss – save that the ever-watchful angel,
in her care and purpose, intervened, and the bike

revved on its way with an angry howl of its horn: moment
in the daylong nightlong of one living, would have been a nothing

to the stately flooding up of eternity... So am I going
back, beyond juggernaut and penny-farthing and cart-wheel,

to a place not-place and a time not-time when Ezekiel's chariot,
its wheels and eyes and wingèd creatures, came thundering,

calling out the power and urgency of God, while I was already
being framed to take into my soul the wisdom of the Good Book,

to have Word and words burning on my lips, spittle-frail
as honeycomb or wasps' nest: to be sentinel, voicing the wonders

of the living creatures and the continents of the cosmos:
for this I was created, and for this saved: but if that motorbike,

veering and swerving...

THE EVENING BREEZE

Adam, the Good Book tells, lived on
nine hundred and thirty years. Finally passed away
into the staggered pages of that good book.

Methuselah stuck it out for some
nine hundred and sixty-nine years
before he learned how to die; but Enoch,

who knew how to walk with God at the time
of the evening breeze, lasted merely three hundred
and sixty-five years before the darkness took him.

Old men. Too many years on the earth. And then
there was Abraham: Abram, Abe. God called him
by his name, told him his own, El Shaddai, God

of the heavenly drumlins. Now they could talk
freely, of wonders, of a child to be born to him
in old age, descendants many as the grains of corn

down all the sorry centuries. Aged one hundred
seventy-five, Abraham, Abram, Abe, breathed his last,
adventurer, one of the youngest of them all.

MOSES AND JOHN-JAMES

Moses, that fiery prophet, discovered on the barren
árdán of Horeb that the tree of life burns on
and the world turns; beloved of old-time Yahweh
he died with the Almighty's fierce embrace about him.

Our neighbour – who lived a long, unspectacular life,
in his cottage inhabited for generations, at the tail end
of a softly shadowed bóithrín, who loved to pause
by the uptangled ditches on the lane-sides – has died,
kissed discreetly on the lips by the gentle Christ,
hearsed up the roads and cattle-lanes he had walked
head high with knowledge and the Mosaic covenant.

These country fields and trodden paths, will admit
each death as they welcome rain, a flight of swans
or the failure of a crop; now the old man follows
along our axis mundi, while the gleaming hearse
pauses by the high ash tree where the red squirrel
carries messages from the hard earth to the tree top.

At crossroads, farm-gate and kitchen door, the people
wait for the cortege to pass, offering homage to something
we are not quite sure of; in our deepest hearts
we greet the ghosts in their generations that wander
quietly about the winter sheds, the dusty summer yards,
and talk old legends, local histories, the promised land.

THE GREEN PLOVER

I am haunted still by that manifest old
regular irregular cranking skreek
from the ill-greased axle of a cart
hauling home its load of harvested peat –
something like the marshland cry of the curlew
or the scream of the just-snared hare. This
turning, turning world! and I on the piano stool,
child-fingers graceless at the scales, contrary
motion and arpeggio. They told me
creation's chronicles have been garbled,
its music a cacophony. So I clung
to the rood of clay I come from, hoping yet
there may be universes of star and light
where angels guide the heavenly spheres
towards an ultimate harmony… I wonder
if the first birth is a death; perhaps the final
death may be a birth and the spirit will set out
on a greater journey, as yet unsatisfied,
down mud-fields and cobbled avenues
of regret. Who is to know if this is yet
the final journey, universe so vast and its
axle maybe rusting, for how can spirit
come to a halt, though it be in the bosom
of Abraham himself? A flight of lapwings now,
green plover, have lifted sudden and erratic
from the marshland fields along the sandbanks,
the waters of Blacksod Bay under rain-mist
and a storm blowing in; their cries are plaintive,
suffering winter and sea-wind sorrow, for they
know well things at their source, unmanifest.

THE RED LINE: DOWNTOWN CHICAGO

In the scareful echo-chambers of the underearth,
where the zinc-can trains come crashing and

thundering through, the gentle and resonant voice
of one of the almost-lost, is offering the song

the angels choired in the night sky above a stable.
Eyes closed he nods in time, beating on his palm

with a child's hand-rattle; red wind-cheater tattered,
bruised bedroom slippers, red Cubs baseball cap –

his song is prayer, is sweetness, he sings as if
conscious of sin, and not expecting coins. Sometimes

the clatter and hustle of arriving and departing trains
devours his voice, his hymn; then, ceasing to sway,

he watches in silence, and sighs as if to say oh
yes, I have compassion still upon the multitude.

SHEPHERD

I had known nothing, felt nothing, held to nothing;
the sky was above, it was sky, the lake dark water,
and the earth hard; I lived with the rough edges
of things, thorny hedge-growth, and my uncouth
companions; we sat, darkling and diminished.
There was talk of a birth, among some lost souls
down the stone-scattered hillside; in dusk-dark,
the sheep were shuffing about, a blackbird chanted
as if the light depended. I watched the owl-quiet
harrier brush over the bushes, heard alarm-calls
from the hidden bird; I worried about the lambs,
out on the upland grasses. But a birth, near hand,
would certainly be diversion. A few of us
threaded our way downhill, blathering: we found
only a bothy, a spluttering lamp, a child, sleeping,
wrapped in rag-things. There was the mother, exhausted,
her lovely face lit with wonder; and the weary-looking
father, a strength contained. Nothing more; crooked,
sagging roof-beams, a floppy scattering of fodder,
a vague, animal smell: nothing that might give a spark
to a dried-out heart, though I sensed a soothing
silence and a peacefulness that hung like warmth
on the dusty air. We were greeted, kindly, and felt
strangely honoured, familial even. Awkward,
with little to say, we returned, and I knew myself
lightened somehow, in a disturbing tranquillity,
aware of the vastness of sky and the multitudinous
shimmering of the stars, the steadfast, slow music
of our dissonant, pastoral and unintelligible days.

THE THREE OF US

We were sitting under the juniper tree, a fatuous
trinity; before us, in the emperor's garden, one
bronze crocus was pushing up; we were bored
with our childish ball-games, with seasonal weathers,
we were aghast at night skies shivering with stars.
Too long the sun seemed nailed to the taut blue
of the sky, yet a sense of darkness pervaded. We
knew such sorrows, wars flooding the plains, leaving
pain and the broadcast seeds of further wars.
Our gods were foolish, fleshless; because we do not live
by reason only, we dreamed of a wisdom to be unearthed
beyond the rim of folly. We would face the challenges
of the unknown. We headed west. Scared, seeking.
We knew the past could never be stitched back together;
the elders, snickering in the corners, told us we would be
joining the community of the irrational. What we found
was a small house, impoverished; an inner room, a child,
mewling, a mother, plainly beautiful, a robust father:
propitious place, contentment, against all reason. Peace,
yet with urgency, a notion of what might be possible, old
simplicity, kindliness and care. We discovered, too,
what seemed a nothingness, a stillness, that yet appeared
an everything, contained. Gifts? No, only our hearts, but we
received much in return. We stayed, knowing ourselves
welcomed. Afterwards we stood outside, exalted;
from a dim corner, a source of light, in our bleak hearts
a galaxy of hope. We were told of Herod, the old dependency
on violence; we turned for home; the sky was clear, the way
straight. We knew the journey would be difficult.

EMERGENCE

A GARDEN ENCLOSED
April, May 2020

See now! ghostly blossoms of the blackthorn
hang along the hedgerows in their motley
off-white nightgowns; there is loveliness
in every matter under heaven, even though
the blackthorn-fruit is thorny-bitter. See, too,
how the early marsh orchid rises in Lenten
purple. Between blackthorn in March and
whitethorn's sacramental innocence in May
we will have suffered such sicknesses and deaths
that grief will be our daily bread, helplessness
our standing. The nights will be startling
when a Paschal moon lifts white as buttermilk
over the pine-trees opposite while the world
lies in unsettling stillness. Two thousand years
and our souls are still small and hard as nubs,
we have not cared sufficiently for the ground
beneath our feet. I reach for comfort: watch
how the furze seeds itself again in chastened gold,
sanctuary for butterfly, stonechat and fox.

*

I stepped down where the roads cross,
there by the three meagre alder trees;
a dutiful donkey rubbed his hide against the bark;

Yeshua Jesus, I prayed,
by whom we are all harrowed, all hallowed,
be with me in this day's task;

high gate-pillars stood without a gate,
shadowed by unruly rhododendron woods;
at the road's edge, lemon-gold of celandine

stood against the black of a discarded tyre.
Here, *Saint Joseph's*; I turned up the avenue,
followed its irksome twists and bends

under the unleafed poplars;
heads of the daffodils were already drooped
and sodden. And then the home:

its watchful windows, its long low stretch,
this old place of old sorrows
still sunlit, decked out in gay attire.

*

In immaculate gardens bright narcissi
stood in loveliness, their sheet-white faces
astonishing, full of grace. In the TV room
a vase of red geraniums was a quivering light;
the vulnerable wait, abstracted, in managed
comforts; body, mind, exquisite faïence,
knocked over; they watch, as children watch,
wide-eyed, and yearn, these frail ones, listless,
for the impossible. Armchairs and frames,
sweet-polished floors, and apart in a far
corner, Great-Aunt Lily, white-haired, stilled.
How brittle they all seem, the bones within
unmaking themselves, the minds of many
unravelling like wool, blotched hands quivering.

*

I had sat alone, last night;
the Paschal moon had risen
over the pine wood, closer to us than before,

lifting through the bare
branches of the trees; soon it was dark
and darkening, and the earth breathed heavily

in the stillness; a dog
yelped in the distance; there fell
a deeper stillness. Or was it fox, calling

to the vixen, or crying out
in pain? Everywhere the invisible
destroying flood, all of us in need of presence

and re-assurance. Strange
outlines under the moon, the lone bush
dark with its ancient, covenanted thorns. Fox,

once beautiful, skulks,
patched bare with mange, betrayed
by our snares and poisons. Now we

move in dread,
knowing how our fractured
hearts, our sundered souls, are

snared, this plague
of deadly, great proportions,
come upon us as if we were born guilty.

*

She sits in an alcove, where the sun will not disturb her;
her eyes are fixed on her fingers, fidgeting slowly
round each other. She sits – not she, the mind closed down,
that lovely face bleak as a cloth, ragged and hanging.

Lord, I pray, now you may dismiss your servant, light
gone out, untreated bruises on her arms and wrists. Here –
an ending that is not ending and how can I offer praise,
or comfort. In her, all humanity is in distress; she waits

in willow stillness, but perhaps Lord Jesus, you call
from across that dark abyss? Or does she stray, alone,
through a rough-cast wilderness? The gold ring
hangs loosely on her finger. She scarce breathes and I

might number all her bones. If you, Lord, are dealing
punishment for humanness, it is the wearied old
that shoulder the heavy beam. I touch her wrist;
there is no response. If I could only weep. . .

*

I have been thinking, Lily, of the *Song of Songs*, and of your
cottage garden – do you remember? – *You are a garden
enclosed, a fountain sealed.* You were young, beautiful, newly
qualified; I saw the people come and go to your surgery and
I loved to watch the bees raid your marigolds, delphiniums,
hydrangeas. Dear Aunt Lily, do you remember the day
I cycled down to visit you? I was, perhaps, ten, the fuchsia
blossomed, the yellowhammer called. I was so proud of
my new red bike, but on your sandy road leading to the
shore, I came tumbling off and yelled with pain, in front
of your small wooden gate; I sat, humbled, holding my
right knee and you came hurrying out. Brave boy, you said,

as you examined me; you went inside and came out
with a bowl of warm water, with cloths, and instru-
ments. It hurt, but very soon, in triumph, you held
up a small silver tweezers and showed me a pebble,
red with blood; I cried again, but you hushed me, you
bandaged up the wound. I sat on. Stunned, embar-
rassed. You laughed; my bike was lodged in the fuch-
sia bushes and you plucked a flower, held my wrist
and squeezed out a small honey-drop onto my skin;
I was distracted, astonished. . . till you bent down
and licked the nectar from my wrist. You laughed
again, then helped me up. I stammered something,
mumbled thanks, pulled up my bike and, mounting
awkwardly, headed for home. Aunt Lily, do you re-
member? She was sitting very still now, eyes fixed on
the window; I hoped that, somewhere inside, some
precious where within her heart, something stirred.
I touched her blemished wrist and whispered: *set me
like a seal upon your heart, like a seal upon your arm. For
love is as strong as death, love no flood can quench, no
torrents drown.*

*

Morning, and the lauds of birdsong; the sudden
saxophone squawk of a pheasant; the day held,

uncertain, self-absorbed. I opened the red gate
onto an empty road; blossoms of the laurel

were a fading brown. The healer has been laid
behind a great stone, dead among the dead. I,

waiting. Not a breeze touched the forest trees.
World is thorned round with terrible injustice

and how can the earth then fail to be enraged?
Cosmos has been in covenant with us, now

meadows have been shorn of rushes, fields
are spread with slurry, in expectation. You, Lord,

are absent, the blood-light that has pulsed inside
the sanctuary has gone out; there is no

sanctuary. Yet now the cuckoo has been calling
somewhere across the valley, finding our hearts

more vulnerable, to respond. I have dreamt
the rooted bones of the long uncountable dead

spread out across a stone-dry land and stirring
under a soft rain, under a word, whispered.

IN THE ONE SPIRIT

The sky was a humming and frosty blue;
at sunset, against the veined and naked
branches of a sycamore, a bulging half-moon –
of jasmine white – insisted; higher than high

a jet-plane left a straggling, pink-orange line
and passed, without a sound, towards elsewhere;

I had thought, all day, of the Holy Ghost,
if, perhaps, the he or she of it could be inveigled
to offer to the thorned heart some rare, grounded
poetry of being, to hold in place that numinous

and sometimes ruinous sense of need we feel
for warmth and certainty, for telling words
to live on a white page in lines that would lighten
the dark, with receptivity, wisdom, love.

THE GATHERING

It is said that those we have loved and lost –
      the million millions who have gone before –

come out at dusk to relish body-time again
      and rush about in most curious murmurations.

Once I heard a high-pitched cry from the birth-room,
      a wail of loss, from the otherwhere and otherwise

and I would have caught the helpless newborn to me,
      enfolded and warmed it but I could not. And once

I heard from somewhere, out in the night, amongst
      junked back-yards and suburban side-ways, a fox, that

once-masterful creature, bark out of his fox-sorrow,
      suffering weathers and bin-lid indignities. I know

we too are but dry bones, bleached and brittle, our hold
      being tenuous, at best. Starlings, they say,

can mimic in song the best a bird can do; but their own
      performances are in massed choirs, at dusk,

flinging themselves in a million millions about the sky,
      sashay-shimmering, a mixum-getherum ruffle-up of wings

before the roost; they form sentences from the afterlife
      that are wholly indecipherable; it looks like night itself

shattering and regrouping, whale shape, dromedary,
    now a heart, fling and furiousness of the mystery;

perhaps it has little to do with roosting, nothing to do
    with wooing, courtship, birthing or dying; perhaps

it is a carefully choreographed ballet of acclaim,
    hosanna, alleluia to the glory of birdhood,

to the wonder of updraft and sky, wings and treetops,
    to the great all-maker who is, in multiple, a starling.

THE MAYFLY

i.m. Donal P. Deane

We have come a long way,
from the virgin snow-drop to the berry red as blood;

always, absence and stillness
are our source and trajectory, so we yearn

for silence,
and a listening deeper than word or thought.

Of all the possibilities – this place, this age, this flesh –
this paltry ego;

high on the ravaged mountain
the winds come sweeping in from the many counties

with ferocity; the skeletal steel masts withstand them,
so, too, the tufts of fine bog-cotton.

Now lilies, gravid and sorrow-white,
wilt on the graves;

we have come a long way, though our being –
wilful, dominant – is ephemeral.

Where it is always a beginning: your naked feet
plosh cool in the silt-mud of the lake bottom,
a misery of slime and ooze, and a broken
shell makes you cry out in pain:
there will be blood, a cut, but you –
faithful to him as you are – get on with it.
He is preparing rod and oars, as you push and grind
the heavy clinker-built row-boat, out from the shore
into deeper water, where it scrapes on sand and then
lolls a while, gracefully, and you hold tight lest it drift
away on the lake water. Father, almost
mythic hero to you, climbs, ungracefully, in. You
follow. A settling, and you sit, gratefully, astern
while he takes the oars, and rows, powerfully, pleased.

The boat touches amongst the reeds, far side the lake,
the prow shush-shushing in and holding;
the high stems, the sedge are still, with only the lake's
soft lapping and the surface so calm you could dream
of walking on the water. Father waits, savouring. Then
he is fishing, the fly-rod long and tapering,
the shush-swish of the line the only sound. You
are content, you, child, to be here with him,
big-built man, muscular, adroit and in control.
There comes, as if out of the stillness, a sudden
commotion on the surface, a stirring, and there lifts
a swarm of the most delicate, insubstantial flies,
grey-white with light-veined lace-curtain wings,
ephemeroptera, hundreds of them, thousands,

as if each drop of water had sprouted wings;
mayfly, by Jove, he whispers, excited, *rising
after years*. It is a hatching from the waterwomb;
some fly low over the surface, as if with destination,
some flutter in place, confused, and many seem
to flounder on the surface; then trout everywhere,
feasting, rising from the water, and splashing back.
He laughs, astonished and awed, as are you,
as if all the stars in all the heavens fell like flakes
and all the fishes of all the seas devoured them. Mayfly,
old as the dinosaur, he says, though the mayfly still
thrive; imago, sub-imago, nymphs and naiads, years
waiting in the bottom silt and lifting, here, today,
to mate and lay and die. The mighty and the meek.

*

He came in from the yard, the door scraping shut
behind him; we heard him in the scullery, washing away
the oil and saw-dust before he came in
to the living-room, no word spoken. We grew
tense in our silences, knowing the signs.
Mother suggested prayers and we knelt, elbows
on the seats of our chairs. I could hear
her green-glass rosary irritate the timbers.
I prayed, child-prayers, not yet knowing all
the words, not knowing prayer is to be found
in the deepest silence. Where truth lies. Waiting.
Afterwards he ranged the living-room floor,
pacing, over and back, back, over, hands joined
behind him, fingers twitching, and we sensed
the struggle, the will wearying, the stout heart
pounding. He stopped, moved rapidly to the door,
and we heard the car starting, the engine revving.

At last, decades older, I sat outside, evening, a tallow
candle-flame smoking against the bugs; the years
are hurrying by, body drags and the limbs ache.
I was picturing Icarus; while his father flew
with reasoned strength, the son aimed high and fell,
fragility of his wings making him a hero. The Sibyl
cautioned Aeneas to honour the gods, and, terrified,
he stood on the threshold of the Underworld,
resolute to filch one final meeting with his father, dead.
Here, in near-dark, a night-bird called from the wood
beyond me, and I sensed the bats whizz-wheeling
round and over me; I stood, finding the trees risen
to threatening presences; then stooped, to touch the earth
for forgiveness. I shivered, and was not cold.

Foot of the bed, he was seated in dressing-gown
and slippers, we, his adult children, hushed
around him. As if we were not there. Nothing
more to offer, his gaze was inwards, words
unwelcome. I sensed the dragging of the weary
body, I knew the struggle within him to free
the spirit from the gravity and cloy of bone
and brain. And I prayed for a charcoal fire, lit
on the lakeshore, to welcome him. The failures,
the suffering, lie as silt clogging the flesh,
and he was ending, emptying himself
into himself. Leaving. I could see a great
hosting round him, with vast swarms rising,
like mayfly, towards the world of light.

*

There came a summer storm, fierce winds swelling
from south, from north, whipping the leaves
and smaller branches from the ash and oak; rain
sluiced down the windows, the smaller birds
were flung about like thistledown. I shut my eyes
and opened my being to the Presence that is beyond
thought and consciousness. But my mind
faltered. And I saw him, in his manliness, striding
the slopes of Slieve More with the winds yowling
round the ledges of the mountain. I called, and –
for a moment – all creation seemed to hesitate;
he shook his head and waved, kindly, then hurried on,
and too soon merged into the landscape, like rock
or tussock, leaving me shaken, bog-cotton in the wind.

We have come a long way, childhood to old age; he
has been gone a long time;

I would have said farewell,
have spoken of addiction, tried to say I love you

but the years of diffidence between us
held me mute;

now I will honour how he turned his face
into the prevailing winds

though falling often, rising, labouring on
against the grain,

head down, eyes narrowed
and the tears, at times, scalding;

there is nowhere now — nowhere save in prayer,
where I might speak with him.

THE TIDE GOING OUT

On Bunnacurry shore, the tide going out, I stand,
a little stooped under the heaviness of years,

somewhat slow of breath, weighed like rippled sand
under streels of weed. Amongst the rocks

I have come upon new wonders, the brittle bone-debris,
the feather-mash of some unidentifiable

sea-bird. I have learned there is no pleasure found
in the loss of any created thing;

even the individual gnat within the scrawling
vast tornado of gnats has its own world-wisdom,

born in time and in time will die. Small green crabs
lurk among tiny and sideways hurdling sand-hoppers

where I paddle, soothing my bones in the forgiving
waters of ocean. But do not ask me to speak

of the wisdom of old men, for it is pooled
in the stony flesh of the heel, and in the heart.

A PLACE APART

If we fall, being smitten, who is there
who will gather us up? And if we are to die,
alone and in distress, who will stand in
among the respirators, the monitors, to offer
presence and a kindly hand? I pray that death

may have touched my mother's brow so softly
her going will have been a small disturbance,
merely one eased out-breathing. There has been

snow all day, a dark but homely falling, the sky
a basin-full turned upside down to let it feather
as it will, and after the snow, I can relish
a new silence, a soft-fall peace. There are times

to seek a quiet place apart, to kneel, perhaps,
on stone, to be shriven. It was when I had lost her

that she touched my heart and entered deeply;
we quarrelled, for she insisted on a catechism
of essential truths, imperatives of order, a crude
locutus est. Now I know it was the age, accepted,
like the frost. I look up at the quartered moon

casting a gentle light over the snow, making
of our one world a twilit loveliness, of ragged
winter hedgerows, of fields of miracle and loss.

TRIPTYCH MIRROR

i.m. Mary Josephine Deane

Darkness encompasses me,
in waves, breaking;
I suffer splashes of light,
like sun-flashes under-water;

wraiths and ghost-like shapes oppress me,
they whisper, they touch my body
with manipulative claws
but I do not know them, for I hover –

another self, like a grey mist –

above them, and above my body which lies prone,
chained to this world with tubes and wires, a steel
crown about my brows, ducts in my throat and nostrils,
and my eyes scalded, unseeing.

They will not let me die.

Once they called me pretty, then beautiful, now
I am withered, a dried-out apricot. I recall
the excitable monk Merton, standing on a street-
corner, who stared at the mickle crowds and said –

you stroll about, but you are shining like the sun.

*

Where my body waits – speck of the speck
that is creation – it is light, and a beautiful rain
falling. It has stilled the high trees beyond my window,

bush and grass and flower raise their faces to it,
extending naked arms; it batters them down, and they exult,
life plashing about them like children at their play.

I thought that the clarities given to me would last
till deathtime and beyond, but I was wrong. I cried
when a storm put out the candles on the chestnut tree.

*

There are photos:

Patty and Jim: on the shore, dancing in the waves;
Patty and I, on the lower slopes of Vesuvius,
glasses of gold-white wine lifted in celebration;

Patty, studio lovely: big eyes, startling, perfect lips;

Patty's grave; the silence of stone; ocean
mourning in the distance.

*

The man I was to love came onto the island,
a stranger, came like a spore on the wind
and settled on my heart. I began to cherish
the looking-glass, the unruffled surface
of a new dream. He came onto the island
bearing the *Sturm und Drang* of Goethe, Schiller,
the wildering steppes of Borodin and Pushkin.
to our quiet, unassuming island. Its yearning.
But there was width and depth and breadth

in our romancing, laughter and objective;
I would have lain down before him, like Ruth
at the feet of Boaz; he would have said,
Your island will be my island, your God
my God. Our days rosebuds, our nights blossoms.

*

Those evenings, when he hadn't come home, I felt
as if wet sand lay on the floor of my belly;
I listened to the rains sobbing across the pines
as the night eked itself away and I sat too long
before the mirror, wondering where on earth
I had gone wrong. Now, after years, I look
down upon my body in its loneliness; Nurse
speaks to me as to a child and I strain
to respond, but eye and tongue and heart do not
co-ordinate and mind asserts no interest;
she scolds me, mildly, knows it is not I
lying here, I am the past and the future only,
the present hangs unsteadily like a water-drop
from a branch reaching out over a river.

*

In my bedroom I gaze into the triptych mirror,
a wizened visage gazing back at me. And there he is, my son,
the difficult one, entering the room, and I know

I have slipped again between cracks, future and past, find
I cannot speak; he is gazing through me, stands
before the mirror; he is looking in the glass but I am not

there and I know that I have died, I am ghost-spirit,
he, too, is ghost. He is picking up the hairbrush, smells the few
grey hairs, lets my green-glass rosary slip

through his hands; I reach out to him, but this is nightmare
and he turns to the door, and is gone. I am there
again in the mirror, chilled, and never so much alone.

*

Advent: season of waiting. A gentle snow
falling. My body slowly growing still. Little
time left. All Eternity. I can hear ice forming
on the lily-lake; I feel light somehow, diffuse
as if my self were dissipating. The man came,
hours ago, to sit by my failing body. Sits now,
a stranger once, and I now, stranger to him. He
takes my hands and folds them over my old
green-glass rosary. Nurse urges him away;
he goes, old man stooped in sorrow, leaves
a kiss on my cold brow. I am, perhaps,

disappearing from the mirror   or
disappearing into it and beyond

                         I am become
the liquid in the bedside-glass the flowers
in the vase on the sick-room's windowsill

                            the vase the windowsill

I am the trees under snow at the lake's edge the
       light
glimmering on the frozen lake,
                   the whitest lily
                      the black water

the mirror, broken

EMERGENCE

After the long sorrows and the upset,
when the rains have stopped and the storms eased,
you will walk out again, the roads still lustrous wet,
you will breast the rise, and pause; listen a while

to the burble of excess rainwater along hidden drains
and the welcoming scold of the wren and chaffinch;
half-hidden at the base of the blackthorn hedge,
a fox-run leads towards the secrecy of a dark wood

and you find, by a solitary ash, where the new grasses
are disentangling from the old on the cramped
ditch-top, an early purple orchid, rising lone
towards pyramidal grandeur and enigma. Stand

for a while in mid-morning silence, to savour
the presence of the world as you knew it, maternal
though strict, embracing and aloof, till you feel part
of the insistent and discreet stirring of new life,

your part being to be yourself, attentive, open
and quietly expectant, aware of the simple desire
to be one with the presence, the stillness, to hold
in acceptance the long sorrows and the loss.

THE ACORN

Turn in then, from the darkening evening,
through the red gate, and see, just there,
the oak tree to your right, tall and elegant,
not old, a presence that holds – in bole
and branches – tradition and a linear
connection, its story one of an acorn
gifted, gathered by the poet Seamus Heaney
from Henry David Thoreau's Walden Pond
in Concord, Massachusetts, and planted
here, in love and memory, to be a spring
of energy and possibility, a spur
and magnitude on a small disordered lawn
and growing well, the way you might hope
that what is best in the world will not succumb
to frosts, or violence or epidemics
or ever be wholly overcome in death –
but will thrive, here, in the peaceable kingdom
as – *walk on air*, I whisper, *walk on air* –
while inside the house of the red gate
there is faithfulness and love, where we
are keeping watch, maintaining light.

THE GATE

Sometimes, towards dusk, when the winds
come buffeting from the east, the Holy Ghost slips in
through the red bars with a loud sigh,
brings a cold shivering near the heart and leaves me
restless. These nights – as the world faces its nightmares

of wars and violence – I think I hear
the reassuring and unsettling surges of the sea –
not the rough, unpredictable waters of Atlantic Ocean
but waves of grasses under the breeze
and gracious meadows wild with buttercups.

When, late evening, I lean on the topmost bar
of the red gate, looking out on the shadowed world,
I search the innermost reaches of the spirit, scared
lest I discover emptiness, a well that has run dry and holds
only woodlice and weevils in its depths;

but then I have swung around with joy
to hear the scratchy song of the whitethroat
as it rises from a fence and flies
low and fast into a field. For the red gate
is frontier and boundary, embrace

of the within and the without, eye of the needle,
its blood-red bars criss-crossing the entrance
into, and out of, life. Inside the gate I release the words
like variegated moths held fluttering in my hands
and hope they will not fly in vain. Sometimes,

after dusk, words failing and darkness swelling
from the woods, I think my spirit may slip out
through the red gate of the sheepfold, will find
the longed-for strength – and with a profound sigh
will soar away towards a long-anticipated rest.

ACKNOWLEDGEMENTS

Agenda (UK), Temenos Academy Review (UK), Image Journal (USA), Presence (USA), Poetry Ireland Review, Cyphers, Irish Times, Southword, RTE Sunday Miscellany, Intercom, International Times (ed. Rupert Loydell), Practical Theology Journal (UK), Irish Catholic, Festschrift for Gerry Murphy, Ekstasis (ed. D.S.Martin), Conversations

The poem 'Franciscan Monastery: Achill Island' was commissioned by and is dedicated to the Franciscan Brothers of the Third Order Regular, on the occasion of their bicentennial (1820–2020), who opened a monastery and school on Achill Island in 1852 and served the island well until 1978. The poem is offered in memory of Vincent English.

The sequence: 'The Corniche Carriage Clock' was published in *Irish Pages*, Volume 11, Number 1: 'The Anthropocene'.

The sequence: 'Of Human Flesh' was published in *Christianity and Literature*, *Vol. 72, 2023*, edited by Richard Rankin Russell and published by Johns Hopkins University Press.